First Facts® PREDATOR PROFILES

# SHARKS

## — BUILT FOR THE HUNT —

by Tammy Gagne

Consultant: Dr. Jackie Gai, DVM
Wildlife Veterinarian

CAPSTONE PRESS
a capstone imprint

First Facts are published by Capstone Press,
1710 Roe Crest Drive, North Mankato, Minnesota 56003
www.capstonepub.com

**Library of Congress Cataloging-in-Publication Data**
Gagne, Tammy, author.
  Sharks : built for the hunt / by Tammy Gagne.
      pages cm. — (First facts. Predator profiles)
  Summary: "Informative, engaging text and vivid photos introduce readers to the predatory lives of sharks"—Provided by publisher.
  Audience: Ages 6-9.
  Audience: K to grade 3.
  Includes bibliographical references and index.
  ISBN 978-1-4914-5037-6 (library binding)
  ISBN 978-1-4914-5081-9 (eBook PDF)
1. Sharks—Juvenile literature. 2. Predatory animals—Juvenile literature. I. Title.
  QL638.9.G225 2016
  597.3—dc23                                    2015006661

**Editorial Credits**
Brenda Haugen, editor; Kazuko Collins and Juliette Peters, designers;
Tracy Cummins, media researcher; Katy LaVigne, production specialist

**Photo Credits**
Corbis: Thomas Kokta/Masterfile, 5; Getty Images: Dr. Klaus M. Stiefel /Pacificklaus Photography, 18, Jens Kuhfs, 21; Minden Pictures: Norbert Wu, 15; National Geographic Creative: NICK CALOYIANIS, 19; Science Source: Georgette Douwma, 17; SeaPics.com: Randy Morse, 7; Shutterstock: Derek Heasley, Back Cover, Matt9122, 13, Cover, Nantawat Chotsuwan, 2, pashabo, Design Element, Shane Gross, 1; SuperStock: NHPA, 3; Thinkstock: Jupiterimages, 11, webguzs, 9.

Printed in the United States of America.
009576R

# TABLE OF CONTENTS

# ON THE HUNT

The mighty shark has spotted a sea lion. The shark moves closer as it circles its **prey**. Before the sea lion even senses any danger, bam! The shark speeds up and rams the helpless animal before eating it. This powerful move often stuns the prey. Sometimes it even kills the prey.

Sharks are known for being at the top of the food chain in oceans. While sharks eat many other animals, few animals eat them. Most sharks eat smaller fish. But some sharks also eat seals. sea lions, and even whales.

## FACT
Thresher sharks swat their tails at small fish to stun them before eating them.

**prey**—an animal hunted by another animal for food

# MANY SIZES

Sharks come in many sizes. Spined pygmy sharks are one of the smallest sharks. They are only about 8 inches (20 centimeters) long. These tiny **predators** rely on their sharp teeth for catching prey such as small squid and shrimp. The blue shark is much bigger. It is about 12.5 feet (3.8 meters) long. It uses its size to overpower sea birds, seals, and turtles.

The great white shark is the biggest predatory fish. It can grow to 20 feet (6 m) long and weigh 4,200 pounds (1,905 kilograms)!

## FACT
The bull shark has the strongest bite of all sharks. It can bite a sea turtle in half, shell and all!

**predator**—an animal that hunts other animals for food

blue shark

# LIFE IN THE FAST LANE

Great white sharks have strong jaws. Few animals can escape the jaws of this powerful predator. Great whites are one of the fastest sharks. When chasing prey, they can swim up to 35 miles (56 kilometers) per hour.

Most sharks hunt alone. But dogfish sharks hunt in a pack like wolves. Sometimes hundreds of sharks work together, attacking prey from below or behind. The other animals have little chance against such a large group.

## FACT

Sharks rarely attack people. Deadly shark attacks only happen about once every two years in the United States.

great white shark

# CUTTING TEETH

Most animals have one row of teeth. Sharks have five to 15 rows of teeth in each jaw. The spiky teeth are used to grab prey. Long, curved teeth prevent slippery fish from escaping. Some teeth are **serrated** like knives. A shark uses these teeth for cutting into its food.

## FACT

Sharks are always growing new teeth. When old ones fall out, new ones move forward into their place. As the shark gets bigger, so do its teeth.

**serrated**—saw-toothed

# SEEK AND FIND

Sharks have **keen** senses. If prey is near, a shark will surely see or smell it. Sharks can see in the dark even better than cats can. This helps sharks see in dark, murky water. But not even their eyesight beats their sense of smell. When searching for food, they use this sense the most.

## FACT

Sharks swing their heads from side to side when hunting. This movement helps them follow the scent of their prey.

**keen**—able to notice things easily

# SPECIAL SENSES

Sharks have many dark dots on their faces. Scientists have found that these **pores** are part of a special sense. All living things give off electricity in the water. A shark's pores allow the predator to feel the electricity of its prey.

## FACT

A shark can feel **vibrations** in the water. The vibrations let the shark know that another animal is approaching.

**pore**—a tiny hole in the skin

**vibration**—a fast movement back and forth

# A FISH OUT OF WATER

A few types of sharks are known for jumping out of the water. Mako sharks are among these skilled athletes. They can leap up to 30 feet (9 m) out of the water. This ability helps them chase prey such as sea birds or fish that jump out of the water.

## FACT

A mako shark's body temperature is several degrees higher than the water around it. This **trait** gives the shark extra energy when chasing prey.

**trait**—a quality or characteristic that makes one animal different from another

# AT HOME IN EVERY OCEAN

Many sharks prefer warm water, but some live in colder areas. Sharks live in every ocean. They can even be found in the Arctic and Antarctic regions. Some sharks **migrate** to warmer regions during the winter. They travel to where prey is most plentiful.

## FACT
Arctic sharks sometimes attack polar bears.

**migrate**—to travel from one place to another on a regular basis

A Greenland shark swims
past an underwater ice ledge.

# NIGHT HUNTERS

Most sharks are **nocturnal**. They hunt at night and during the early morning when prey fish are most active. Sharks also tend to move closer to land during these hours. If a shark finds a school of fish, it will often follow it toward the shore.

## FACT

Sharks sleep by resting half of their brain at a time. This allows them to be alert at all times.

**nocturnal**—active at night and resting during the day

## AMAZING BUT TRUE!

Sharks can sense when a hurt animal is nearby. Sharks can smell a single drop of blood in 25 million drops of ocean water. These fierce animals will even attack other wounded sharks.

# GLOSSARY

**keen** (KEEN)—able to notice things easily

**migrate** (MYE-grayt)—to travel from one place to another on a regular basis

**nocturnal** (nok-TUR-nuhl)—active at night and resting during the day

**pore** (POR)—a tiny hole in the skin

**predator** (PRED-uh-tur)—an animal that hunts other animals for food

**prey** (PRAY)—an animal hunted by another animal for food

**serrated** (SER-ay-tid)—saw-toothed

**trait** (TRAYT)—a quality or characteristic that makes one animal different from another

**vibration** (vye-BRAY-shuhn)—a fast movement back and forth

# READ MORE

**Arnold, Tedd.** *Fly Guy Presents: Sharks.* Fly Guy. New York: Scholastic Inc., 2013.

**Guillain, Charlotte.** *Shocking Sharks.* Walk on the Wild Side. Chicago: Raintree, 2013.

**Peterson, Megan Cooley.** *Sharks.* Smithsonian Little Explorers. North Mankato, Minn.: Capstone Press, 2014.

# INTERNET SITES

FactHound offers a safe, fun way to find Internet sites related to this book. All of the sites on FactHound have been researched by our staff.

Here's all you do:

Visit *www.facthound.com*

Type in this code: 9781491450376

**Super-cool stuff!**

Check out projects, games and lots more at
**www.capstonekids.com**

# CRITICAL THINKING USING THE COMMON CORE

1. Make a list of the abilities that make sharks powerful predators. Which ability do you think matters most? (Key Ideas and Details)

2. How would the teeth shown on page 11 help a shark catch prey? (Craft and Structure)

# INDEX